ON EGO

Mick Gordon and Paul Broks

ON EGO

A Theatre Essay

inspired by the book
Into the Silent Land
by Paul Broks

OBERON BOOKS
LONDON

First published in 2005 by Oberon Books Ltd
521 Caledonian Road, London N7 9RH
Tel: 020 7607 3637 / Fax: 020 7607 3629
e-mail: info@oberonbooks.com
www.oberonbooks.com

Reprinted with textual revisions 2006.

A catalogue record for this book is available from the British
Library.

ISBN: 1 84002 609 X / 978-1-84002-609-2

theatre *n.* 1 A building designed for the performance of plays, operas, etc. 2 The writing or production of plays. 3 A setting for dramatic or important events. [From Latin *theatrum,* from Greek *theatron,* place for viewing.]

essay *n.* 1 A short literary composition dealing with a subject analytically or speculatively. 2 To attempt or endeavour; effort. 3 To test or try out. [From Old French *essaier,* to attempt.]

Contents

How does the brain create
a sense of self?

The cognitive scientist David Chalmers calls it 'the hard problem': how do physical processes in our brains give rise to subjective experience? The neuropsychologist and writer Paul Broks puts it another way: how does the kilo and a half of meat you call your brain become your mind?

It is, perhaps, the greatest scientific and philosophic question of all. It asks us to think about what we are, beyond our skin and bone and our hundred billion brain cells. It wonders how the conscious 'you' clambers from the numb darkness of the brain box out into a world of people and places, pleasure and pain, love and loss. It wants to know who 'you' are.

The answer is disconcertingly simple: not who you think you are. Paul Broks, in his beautiful book, *Into the Silent Land, Travels in Neuropsychology*, gently reveals the mistake we so instinctively make about ourselves: our assumption that the first person singular pronoun, 'I', describes a unified self.

> I wake up in the morning; I go to work; I feel happy when things go well and I feel frustrated when they don't; I hold certain beliefs and I express various opinions; I used to like Beethoven but now I prefer Mozart; I like chocolate better than cheesecake; I enjoy walks in the country-side; I take the view that people should be kind to one another, and I feel bad if I do the wrong thing. I act, I feel, I think, I believe, I grow older and I change in other ways. But 'I' am always there at the centre of things. But what is this 'I'? The experiencer of experiences? The thinker of thoughts? The doer of deeds? The simple fact is that there is no 'I' beyond the 'I' of grammar.

This, of course, is very difficult to accept.

Try another approach. As you are reading this you are more than likely hearing a little voice coming from inside your head. Now think: whose is that little voice? Is it yours? Is it mine? Now recall a recent argument that you've had with a loved one. Has another voice arrived? Your lover's perhaps? Your mother's? Listen for a moment. Replay the argument. Hear their criticism and try to remember your reply. Now there are two voices in there – or maybe a third has started to commentate, 'I'm still right!' So who are they, these voices? And who is it that is continuing to read this while they're busy with their altercation? Who is 'you'?

The fact is, we are divided and discontinuous and the mental processes underlying our sense of self – feelings, thoughts, memories – are scattered through different zones of the brain. There is no central core, no special point of convergence, no essence, no ego, no 'I'. We come together – when we do – in a work of fiction. Our brain is a story-telling machine and the 'self' is a story.

But, as has been said, this is very difficult to accept. And it is this difficulty that inspired this theatre essay.

Mick Gordon

Characters

ALEX
a lecturer, mid-thirties

DEREK
a professor, late fifties

ALICE
an interior designer, mid-thirties

On Ego was first performed at Soho Theatre on 30 November 2006, with the following cast:

ALEX, Elliot Levey

ALICE, Kate Miles

DEREK, Robin Soans

Director Mick Gordon

Designer Es Devlin

Lighting Designer Linus Fellbom

Film Honey Brothers

Music Luke and Stephens

Scene 1

A theatre. To the back a screen. ALEX's face on the screen. ALEX enters.

ALEX: Okay, I think we should make a start now.

House lights fade.

And to start with, can I ask you all to please look at me. At my face. This one.

Lights close in on ALEX's face.

What do you see? When you look at my face, what do you see?

Beat.

I'll tell you what you don't see. What you don't see – unless I tell you how to look – what you don't see are the facts of the matter. You don't notice, at first, that my face – any face – is really just an animated device attached to the outer surface of a bony box. But that's what it is.

Knocks top of bony box and demonstrates the animated device with random movements, emotional expressions etc.

It works this way because just below the surface you have these bands of fibre tugging your tissues this way and that and these fibres are stimulated by electrochemical impulses that shoot down from deep inside the box. There's also a hinged structure here and when it lowers it opens up a gaping hole. Then you have a protruding construction in the central region, with two vents, and these deep cavities up here on either side. There's a mobile spherical structure stuffed into each of them. Now this is very odd. If you poke the side of one of these spherical structures – very gently – the whole world wobbles. (*He gently pokes his eye.*) Round to the side you have these things... Try as you might you won't actually see them but you can feel them alright – all curly and folded and if you wear glasses, you'll appreciate that these rather odd structures are perfectly placed to support the arms of your spectacle frames (*Puts on glasses.*) – evidence as good as any for intelligent design.

Lights up.

So, what do you see, when you look at my face, if not the bony box and the mechanical things? You see a *person*. You catch my eye and you see the gleaming signal of consciousness. A *person*. You imagine some ethereal space beneath the vault of my skull, lit by shifting patterns of feeling and thought, charged with intention. A *person*. Behind every face – we think – there is a self. An essence, an ego, an 'I'.

The illusion is irresistible. Why so? Well, we see, we hear and we speak through the face and it also displays our feelings, so we have the impression that consciousness – the stuff of self-awareness – is located in the same region. And, of course, where the box goes, you go. It's undeniable isn't it: you're in there somewhere? And if you're in your box you imagine that other, similar, boxes must also be inhabited. Well they aren't.

Beat.

Look in the space behind the face. Now what do you see?

On the screen, we enter through the eye and into a brain operation.

The fact is there's nothing but material substance: flesh and blood, bone and brain. You look down into an open head, watch the brain pulsate, watch the surgeon tug and probe. And you understand with absolute conviction that there's nothing more to it. There's no one there. Nobody home. No essence, no ego, no 'I'.

Beat.

It's a kind of liberation.

The screen now shows images of brain scans.

Like the surface of the earth, the brain is pretty much mapped. There are no secret compartments inaccessible to the surgeon's knife or the gaze of the brain scanner. There is nothing you can't touch or squeeze, weigh and measure, like any other object. There is no ghost in the machine... just a machine.

On the screen, images of interconnecting neurons.

The machine is awesome. It contains a hundred billion neurons. And each of these neurons is linked to as many as ten thousand others which means there are potentially more possible patterns of connection in your brain than there are atoms in the known universe. Can you imagine? Look close. Shrink yourself down to the size of a brain cell. Enter your own head. Picture yourself perched like a monkey in the jungle of connections. Take a good look around. There's not a spark of colour or whisper of sound. Where are your feelings and thoughts? Where are your hopes and fears? Your memories? Where are you? The jungle is dark and all is quiet.

The screen goes black. Beat.

It's hard to fathom. Really it is. We want to believe there's more to us than that. More than just a mass of tiny robotic cells. How can we possibly accept 'The Astonishing Hypothesis'?

On the screen, the quote. ALEX recites it.

'...that "you", your joys and your sorrows, your memories and your ambitions, your sense of personal identity and free will, are in fact no more than the behaviour of neurons. That conscious experience is not caused by the behaviour of neurons, it is the behaviour of neurons.' Francis Crick.

Enter DEREK carrying a bucket.

DEREK: Your special effect.

ALEX: Great.

DEREK: In a bucket.

ALEX: Sorry?

DEREK: Poor soul dragged down to a watery doom.

ALEX: Thank you Derek.

Exit DEREK. ALEX waits for him to leave then fishes a brain out of the bucket and holds it in the palm of his hand. He considers it.

So how does meat become mind?

Beat.

When I first held a human brain in the palm of my hand I felt…ambivalent. The fascination! But also a little distaste.

I was surprised by how heavy it felt. Perhaps a part of me had expected it to be weightless, like a mental image or a train of thought. We never feel the weight of our own head, do we? It just seems to float there like a thought bubble.

It was a dissection class and I wanted to slice this brain apart and look inside. But I felt reluctant to start cutting – Why? Was it a sacrilege? I imagined the worlds bound in this nut-shell. Sun, moon, sky, clouds, people, places, pleasure, pain, knowledge, beauty, right and wrong. Love and loss. Visible and invisible things. An entire universe, an infinite space stuffed inside this kilo and a half of meat. A lump of meat.

About to put the brain back in the bucket.

Oh, this was Richard, by the way. Volunteered his post-mortem services especially for this. Nice fella. Bit of an extrovert. Round of applause for Richard… No, no, only joking. Though I'm sure he would have loved it.

Puts brain back into bucket.

So how do we get from that (*Points to bucket.*) to this…rich conscious self-awareness we all seem to float around in? The greatest scientific and philosophical riddle of all: How does the brain construct a self?

It's tempting to go back to our intuitive *ego theory* – the assumption that within the machine, behind the structure we call a face, there lurks an ego, an essence an 'I'. The experiencer of our experiences, working the controls, steering the body through the world. But it is an illusion. Our actions and experiences are not owned by some inner essence. Actions and experiences are all we are!

Each life is just a long series or *bundle*, of interconnected sensations and thoughts. And the mental processes underlying our sense of self – feelings, thoughts, memories – are scattered through different zones of the brain. There is no special point of convergence. No central core. We come together in a work of fiction. Our brain is a story-telling machine. And the 'self' is a story.

But it's very difficult to accept, this *bundle theory*. Instinctively we demand: If the self is a story then who tells the story of the self? That's like asking, who thunders the thunder, or rains the rain. It's not so much a question of us weaving the story as the story weaving us.

DEREK brings on a metal stand with a green button on it. He doesn't put it down.

Just there thanks.

DEREK: And have you finished with Richard?

ALEX: Yes. Thank you.

DEREK exits with the bucket.

Can you accept the fact that you are just a bundle of sensations and thoughts or are you too attached to the *illusion* of the ego? Are you an ego theorist or a bundle theorist? Not sure? Try this thought experiment.

The screen now advertises a free trip in a teleporter.

Imagine that you are offered a free trip, anywhere you want to go, in a teleporter. You know, like Star Trek.

You step inside the teleportation chamber.

Lights change, forming a separate area around the stand with the green button.

In front of you, you can see a monitor with the smiling face of the teleporter operator.

DEREK's unsmiling face appears on the screen behind ALEX. ALEX takes a quick look at the screen behind him and smiles.

Hello Derek.

DEREK doesn't reply.

And a green button. If you press it you will begin a sequence of events. Scanners will plot the exact co-ordinates of every atom in your body, encode the information and transmit it to your destination. When the information arrives it will be decoded and you will be replicated – down to the last molecule. So your every memory; your every conscious and unconscious thought travels with you.

DEREK: Going anywhere nice?

ALEX: Sorry?

DEREK: I said, going anywhere nice?

ALEX: Yes, actually. I'm going to have dinner with my wife.

DEREK: Well that is nice. Very nice. Lovely in fact. Do send her my best.

ALEX: Your best?

DEREK: Please.

ALEX: Okay Derek. I'll send her your best.

One final detail: during the scanning process your present body will be vaporised. Totally destroyed. But don't worry, it's completely painless and you'll be perfectly replicated – the instant the signal reaches your destination.

Beat.

So would you press the green button? Would you be happy to be teleported. If your answer is yes, then like me, you are a proud bundle theorist. You understand that you are a complex fluctuating pattern of physiological and mental states, nothing more. Teleportation poses no threat to your identity. You rest assured that your essence, your ego, your inner 'I' won't be destroyed by vaporisation and replication because...well because you have no essence, no ego, no 'I'.

Excuse me; but really, if you're an ego theorist, if you're one of those people who wouldn't press the button, why not? Your replica will be exactly the same as your vaporised original. So what's your objection? What's your rational objection? There is none...unless you believe in...you know...the spooky stuff.

Which of course we all do a little. We're all prone to a little magical thinking. It makes the world go round. It's a bit like...well, suppose someone takes my wedding-ring. They say, 'Look – I'll get you a perfect replica. You can have that.' I'd say: 'No, give me my original wedding-ring back.' 'But look,' they say, 'here's the replica: see, it's exactly the same. Exactly. Take it.' I'd refuse. And they say, 'Well here's the deal: accept the identical copy and I'll give you a hundred pounds to go with it.' 'No,' I'd say. 'Two hundred.' 'No.' 'Three.' 'No, no, no. I want my one and only original, unique wedding-ring back.' 'Okay,' they say, 'here it is.' And I'm relieved. I'm happy. I put the ring back on my finger and I cherish it. But then they say they have a confession to make. They got the rings mixed up. They can't actually be sure it's the original. So now, I'm angry and confused. Why? Magical thinking. I've invested this idea of 'the original' with some strange mystical quality. Utterly irrational. If they hadn't told me of the mix up I'd be none the wiser. Well it's the same as our attachment to the idea of the self: the mystical ego, the essence, the inner 'I'. Utterly irrational.

DEREK: Ready.

ALEX: Can you let go of the illusion? Ready.

DEREK: Okay.

Wait. Then ALEX presses the green button. The scanning begins as lights brighten around him, the screen runs the lecture we have just seen at top speed. Then he waits but nothing happens. ALEX looks confused. He turns round as DEREK says:

DEREK: Shit!

Beat.

Shit, shit, shit.

ALEX: Is there a problem Derek?

DEREK is frantically checking all his instrumentation.

ALEX: Derek, is there a problem?

DEREK looks from his consul to ALEX. For the first time DEREK is smiling.

DEREK: Something extraordinary has happened.

Blackout.

Scene 2

Side room on a neurology ward. ALICE undergoing a neurological consultancy. She sits alone on stage facing the audience. Responding to a test from an unseen, unheard doctor.

ALICE: My name? My name! Oh, come on! It's there in your notes... Wednesday... Wednesday the twenty-second of October... Yes of course I know the year. Trust me, I know it... About four-thirty... Yes, I know the name of the building we're in... Yes, that too... Backwards? ...DLROW.

An unheard question asked.

Yes. I was in the bedroom with my husband. An ordinary morning, I'm early, he's late. It was last Tuesday. And he wanted help choosing his tie. He held two up. And one had stripes and the other had checks. 'Which one?' And I couldn't remember the word for checks. 'Which one?' Nothing – totally blank. 'Alice! Which tie?!' And rather than saying, 'Oh God, sorry I've gone completely blank, what's the word for that one?' I said, 'Not stripes.' And that struck me as odd. I mean it was odd: 'Not stripes.' Don't you think? Eight days ago. The fourteenth.

The following sequence of words now appears on screen, repeating over and over. ALICE is trying to remember them. CLOCK. TABLE. UMBRELLA. KNIFE. TREE. STORM. TRAIN. BOOK. FISH. FLOWER. KITE. OCEAN. BOLT. TRUMPET. PILLOW.

Clock. Table. Umbrella... Tree. Storm. Ocean. Fish. Trumpet...

Beat.

Clock. Table. Umbrella. Knife. Tree. Storm... Ocean... Fish... Leaf. Bed. Pillow.

Beat.

Clock. Table. Umbrella. Knife. Tree. Storm. Train. Flower...Leaf. Rain. No, storm. Did I say storm? Did I say that already? Storm. Ocean. Pillow. Bed. Trumpet!

Another question.

Words beginning with 'F'?

(*Haltingly.*) Flower. Fff... Feather... Flute... Flame... Fog...
(*Long pause, looks at finger.*) Finger... (*Looks at foot.*) Foot...
(*Touches face.*) Face...

Beginning with 'A'?

Ant... Antelope... (*Pause. She is concentrating but her mind is
blank.*) Oh this is ridiculous! ... Anchovy... Atom... Any
word? ... Any at all?... And...

'S'...right... Sugar... Shit (*Smiles.*) I'm sorry. Sugar and shit
seems to be about it I'm afraid.

No, really. I'm alright.

Four-legged animals? Let's see. Dog, Cat, Lion, Tiger...
Horse, Cow... Cat (*Pause.*) I'm sorry. I'm having problems
with this one. Four-legged animals. For some reason I can
only think of three-legged animals... No, I'm joking. Don't
put that in your notes.

Vegetables? No, sorry. Sorry. Actually I think I have had
enough now. I never was any good at games.

Thanks. Thank you.

As ALICE stands, blackout.

Scene 3

*A cell with a table and two chairs. DEREK enters carrying a file and
a mobile phone.*

DEREK: Don't be alarmed.

ALEX gets up, eyes fixed on DEREK.

ALEX: Where am I?

DEREK doesn't reply.

Where am I?

DEREK: Something extraordinary has happened.

ALEX: What's going on?

DEREK: Sit down. (*DEREK sits.*) Actually, you should find this fascinating. And don't worry, there is a solution. Look. Sit down. Then you can consider your position.

ALEX remains standing.

ALEX: How long have I been in here?

DEREK: There's been a problem with the teleportation system.

ALEX: Well clearly.

DEREK: No, no. A real problem.

ALEX: Well how long's it going to take? You know what tonight is. If you're doing this on purpose Derek.

DEREK: No. Absolutely not! Nothing to do with it. But there are implications. Really Alex I do think you should sit down.

ALEX: Is that my phone?

DEREK: Yes.

ALEX: (*Takes the phone.*) Where was it? I thought I'd lost it.

DEREK: Alex, before you dial.

ALEX: What went wrong? I pushed the button but nothing happened.

DEREK: So it appeared.

ALEX: The scanner failed?

DEREK: No, the body scan was perfect.

ALEX: So there was a transmission problem...

DEREK: Not exactly.

ALEX: But I'm not where I'm supposed to be.

ALEX dials.

DEREK: Look I really think you shouldn't...

ALEX: I'm going to be late. Shit. Alice is going to kill me.

DEREK: Not so much.

ALEX: Since when have you been an expert on Alice?

DEREK: No no, I didn't mean that, I meant you shouldn't be too late.

ALEX: What are you talking about?

DEREK: You've been teleported.

Beat.

ALEX: What?

DEREK: You've been teleported.

ALEX: I've been teleported?

DEREK: Mapped and sent.

Beat.

ALEX: What?

DEREK: And you've arrived.

ALEX: Arrived?

DEREK: Safe and sound.

ALEX: But I'm still here.

DEREK: That's the problem.

Beat.

ALEX: But that's impossible. I mean that's...

Beat.

I've been duplicated.

Beat.

I've been duplicated?

DEREK: Yes.

ALEX: (*Smiling. Stunned.*) Well, fuck me.

ALEX looks at the phone.

It's ringing.

Scene 4

On screen, butterflies. ALICE is sitting. On the table beside her, her mobile phone.

ALICE: I could tell straight away it was bad news. 'Do you have anyone with you?' he said. I didn't. Alex was in New York. The doctor sat me down. 'We have your pictures here,' he said, like he was returning my holiday snaps. He was talking about the MRI. And then he clipped a big square film onto the light-box and I was looking into my brain. It was mostly grey and murky, but he pointed out a brighter patch near the middle. 'Look here,' he said, 'and here, and here.' He was tracing shapes across the film and now I could see angel wings. 'What is it?' I said. 'It's a butterfly glioma,' he said. A butterfly glioma! It sounded rather beautiful. 'A tumour,' he said.

A restaurant with a wonderful view. A table and two chairs by the window.

ALEX: Sorry sweetheart.

ALICE: You're alright. I was early.

ALEX: What time is it? I lost my phone again.

ALICE: Again?

ALEX: I'm sure I had it this morning. I think I'm going mad. Sorry…

ALICE: It's alright.

ALEX: I didn't…

ALICE: It's okay.

ALEX: I'm just trying…

ALICE: Very trying.

ALEX: Sorry.

ALICE: Shut up! Happy Anniversary.

ALEX: Yeah. Yeah. Don't know about you but I need a drink.

ALICE: First sensible thing you've said.

ALEX kisses ALICE then goes to fetch drinks.

(*To audience.*) I said, 'Can it be cured?' 'No.' 'Well, can you operate?' 'No. The tumour is inoperable.' Then do you know what I said? I said, 'So how long have I got? How long have I got?' How long have I got, doc, give it to me straight. They never give it to you straight. Even the worst news comes gift-wrapped. You might be devastated but you always seem to leave with a faint sense of gratitude.

ALEX returns with two flamboyant cocktails. ALICE laughs. He gives one to her. They clink glasses and take a sip. They're strong.

How was the lecture?

ALEX: Good. We did the teleporter thing.

ALICE: And how was Dad?

ALEX: (*Delighted.*) Absolutely furious! Someone didn't turn up so he had to assist me!

ALICE: (*Smile.*) I hope you didn't enjoy it too much.

ALEX: He started to ad-lib. The old bastard was trying to upstage me.

ALICE: He just gets anxious when he's not in control.

ALEX: No, no. He knew exactly what he was doing. He still treats me like a student. He thinks I'm cocky.

ALICE: You are cocky.

ALEX: He thinks I'm too cocky.

ALICE: You are too cocky.

ALEX: Because he keeps treating me like a student. He sent you his love by the way.

ALICE: His love?

ALEX: Mmm. I hate to say this, but…

ALICE: Don't…

ALEX: Maybe you should call him.

ALICE looks at him. A moment hangs.

ALEX: No sorry. Sorry, you're right. Of course you are. What am I defending him for? Absolutely. He's a… How did someone as beautiful as you come from someone as wierd as him.

ALICE: Nearly.

ALEX: You look wonderful by the way.

ALICE: Better.

ALEX: You do look wonderful by the way.

ALEX looks at her. He adores her. A small toast.

Sorry. To us.

ALICE: Yes.

ALEX: Yes.

They drink.

I love this place. Best view in town.

ALICE: …

Beat. ALEX looks at ALICE.

ALEX: Sweetheart? Best view in town…

ALICE: Alex [*no…*]

ALEX: Come on it's tradition.

ALICE: Last night you didn't approve of tradition.

ALEX: I didn't approve of believing in things just because they're old. This is totally different. This is good tradition.

ALICE: You're a bully.

ALEX: You love it… Like I love this place because it has the best view in town.

ALICE: Oh, okay, okay! Wow Alex, it's *beautiful.*

ALEX: I knew you'd love it. Look! A shooting star.

ALICE: You made that up. There was no shooting star.

ALEX: How can you say that? It was wonderful. Perfect.

ALICE: There was no shooting star.

ALEX: Candle-light, music, the city glimmering below us, you were looking fabulous, I was looking like me and to top it all a shooting star, *our* shooting star. It was the most romantic night of your life.

ALICE: (*Mimicking ALEX.*) Did you know that shooting stars are *actually* the remnants of comets…

ALEX: That's not funny.

ALICE: (*Continues impression.*) If a shooting star is brighter than the apparent magnitude of Venus, then it may be called a fireball or a bolide. Romantic! It was like going out with an A-level physics book.

ALEX: You have a very nasty side to you.

ALICE: Bolide! Who says 'bolide' before proposing?

ALEX: (*Very seriously.*) I was trying to make an impression.

ALICE: And you think my Dad's weird.

They look at one another. Love.

Do the poem.

ALEX: I can't remember it.

ALICE: (*Mimicking again.*) I can't remember it!

ALEX: Alice…

ALICE: No, it's alright, please.

ALEX: 'The brain is wider than the sky,
　　For put them side by side,
　　The one the other will include,
　　With ease, and you, beside.
　　The brain is deeper than the sea,
　　For, hold them, blue to blue,
　　The one the other will absorb,
　　As sponges, buckets, do.'

Emily Dickinson.

ALICE: Now that was impressive. Now go on, finish it.

ALEX: Don't know the rest.

ALICE: Liar.

ALEX: Honestly, I can't remember.

ALICE: Pathetic.
　　'The brain is just the weight of God
　　For, heft them, pound for pound,

And they will differ, if they do,
As syllable from sound.'

ALEX: There's nothing like God to fuck up a poem.

ALICE: As I said, pathetic.

ALEX: No I'm serious. You can't do it. It's dangerous, it's deluded.

ALICE: You're the one who's deluded.

ALEX: Yes I am. We all are. The problems start when we don't admit it. It's one thing for people to *knowingly* believe in illusions – societies need wise fictions as well as scientific truths – but when we start believing the illusions to be real we're all fucked because brains tell bodies to fight for what's real, and in the case of the delusion we call belief in God, the last two thousand years shows precisely how constructive that can be. Sorry, I know I'm off on one but I do have a point.

ALICE: Several.

ALEX: All I'm saying is, brains make gods, not the other way around.

ALICE: Are you sure that's not what she meant?

ALEX: Who?

ALICE: Emily Dickinson.

ALEX reconsiders for a moment.

I would have liked a violinist.

ALEX: Bollocks. *Hand.*

ALICE gives his her hand.

This is where I closed the deal.

ALICE: Closed the deal?! Have you been talking to those Americans again?

ALEX: Alice Elizabeth Blatchley…

ALICE: You were standing up.

ALEX: Was I?

ALICE: You always stand up when you get excited.

ALEX: Do I?

ALICE: Or nebulous.

ALEX: Nervous.

ALICE: That's what I said.

ALEX: No, you said 'nebulous'. I think you meant 'nervous'.

ALICE: (*Stab of anxiety.*) Oh God…

ALEX: No, it's nothing.

ALICE: Fuck. Alex.

ALEX: No. A slip of the tongue. That's all. Seriously sweetheart.

ALICE composes herself.

ALICE: Yeah. Yeah. Course. I'm going to get us another drink. I'm alright.

ALICE exits taking the two empty cocktail glasses. ALEX looks on. He is extremely concerned. ALICE's mobile rings. ALEX answers.

ALEX: Hello?

DEREK enters. Lights change. We are now back in the cell. ALEX looks at him then hands him the phone. DEREK presses a button, ending the call. ALEX has to sit down.

DEREK: There is a further complication or indeed opportunity depending on one's frame of mind. The creation of surplus individuals is anathema. We can't have random proliferation of persons.

ALEX looks at DEREK. He doesn't understand.

There are certain protocols here. And in this type of case, we recommend that the existence of surplus individuals be discontinued.

ALEX: Discontinued?

DEREK: Yes.

ALEX: I see. How can two people live one life?

DEREK: Precisely.

ALEX: So you're going to...kill...

DEREK: *(Sharp intake of breath.)* That's a very harsh way of putting it and actually technically inaccurate. Anyway, nothing can be done without consent.

ALEX: Have you told him yet?

Beat.

DEREK: We'll come to that.

ALEX: Do not go gentle into that good night.

DEREK: Yes... Um... This is going to come as a shock, but I think I can explain it in a way you'll understand.

ALEX: I'm not one of your undergraduates Derek.

DEREK: I'll put it as simply as I can. Suppose your journey had gone according to plan. Right? You would have stepped into the teleportation booth, pressed the button and initiated the sequence; mapping, encoding, vaporisation, transmitting, yes? And you would have arrived, been decoded and reconstituted.

Beat.

And you would have walked away.

Beat.

Got on with your business. You were having dinner with my daughter I believe.

ALEX: I'm celebrating my wedding anniversary with my wife.

DEREK: Is this what would have happened, yes or no?

ALEX: I don't understand.

DEREK: What I'm trying to explain to you is that this is *precisely* what has happened except this time the vaporisation stage has been a little...delayed.

Beat. ALEX looks, as in his imagination ALICE enters with drinks.

ALICE: Sorry about that sweetheart.

DEREK: That really, there's no difference.

ALICE: I'm feeling very emotional this evening.

DEREK: The experience is always the same.

ALICE: Must be the cocktails.

ALICE reaches for her glass smiling. She drinks then looks at the view.

DEREK: That each time you travel there's perfect continuity between the person dematerialising and the person re-emerging. Perfect continuity.

ALICE: That wasn't there before.

DEREK: Can't you see it...? The twelfth time you travelled you remembered the eleventh, the eleventh time the tenth, and so on. And each time you could reflect not just on that day's events but on events of the previous day, too, and the previous weeks and months and all the years of your life.

ALICE: Max was sick again.

DEREK: Perfect continuity.

ALICE: All over the new carpet.

DEREK: When you looked in the mirror, did you ever say, wait a minute this isn't really me?

ALICE: I think we should take him to the vet.

DEREK: And when you returned home, did Alice ever accuse you of being an impostor? Of course not. Because the man who returned was always the man who had left. The very same man.

ALICE: I could do it tomorrow afternoon, unless you've got time in the morning.

DEREK: But now, because of that delay...

ALICE: Alex?

DEREK: Your replica's experience has gone beyond yours...

ALICE: Alex?

DEREK: So he's not the surplus.

ALICE: Alex?

DEREK: You are.

Beat. Then DEREK exits and we are back in the restaurant.

ALICE: You're miles away.

ALEX: Sorry.

ALICE: Max?

ALEX: Absolutely.

ALICE: Could you take him?

ALEX: Who?

ALICE: Max! To the vet!

ALEX: I don't know. How's the carpet?

ALICE: Completely fine.

ALEX: Is it?

ALICE: Ruined.

ALEX: That little shit. He did it on purpose. He hates me that dog.

ALICE: Max does not hate you.

ALEX: He hates me. He wants me out. Every time your back's turned: (*ALEX does an impression of MAX growling.*) He's as bad as your father.

ALICE: Oh stop being so paranoid. Where were we? We've done the view, we've done the bolide, we've done the poem, we've done the lecture. Bring on 'The Astonishing Hypothesis'!

ALEX: Oh fuck this. Let's just celebrate.

ALICE: No. It's tradition. Woo me as only you can.

ALEX: Alice [No....]

ALEX: Go on, Francis Crick me...

ALEX: Francis Crick...

ALICE: And kneel down. You were kneeling down.

ALEX gets down on one knee.

ALEX: Francis Crick – who was better known as co-discoverer of the structure of DNA – said, that your sense of personal identity, is not caused by the behaviour of neurons, it is the behaviour of neurons. It's an astonishing idea and that's why he called it 'The Astonishing Hypothesis'.

ALICE: Astonishing.

ALEX: Yes it is. But it's not nearly as astonishing...

ALICE: Astonishing.

ALEX: Are you taking the piss?

ALICE: (*Laughing.*) No I'm agreeing with you.

ALEX: Well…why?

ALICE: Because it is astonishing. I agree. Me and the
Bodhisattva.

ALEX: Oh please…

ALICE: 'This bundle of elements is void of Self,
In it there is no sentient being…'

ALEX: You are not a Buddhist.

ALICE: 'Just as a set of wooden parts
Receives the name of carriage,
So do we give to elements
The name of fancied being.'

ALEX: I hate it when you do this. You are not a Buddhist.

ALICE: I should have married James Carson. He was really
nice to me. He was a Buddhist.

ALEX: James Carson was a fake.

ALICE: He taught me how to chant.

ALEX: He was a charlatan.

ALICE: Om Mane Padme Hum.

ALEX: I can't believe you fell for it.

ALICE: Lynette Fraser.

ALEX: What?

ALICE: Lynette Fraser. She wore a lot of beads.

ALEX: That's totally different.

ALICE: Helen with the bendy leg.

ALEX: Now you're being ridiculous, you're not comparing
like with like. Helen did not have a bendy leg.

ALICE: What was her nickname Alex?

ALEX: Helen did not have a bendy leg.

ALICE gives ALEX her ring.

ALICE: Come on. Here. Get back down.

ALEX: You've put me off.

ALICE: Apologies Grasshopper.

ALEX: Stop it.

ALICE: But it's not nearly as astonishing…

ALEX takes the ring and kneels down.

ALEX: But it's not nearly as astonishing…as truly, completely, absolutely, completely, astonishing…as you.

ALICE: You said completely twice.

ALEX: What do you expect, I was very nebulous.

ALICE: Alex!

He produces her ring.

ALEX: Will you marry me?

ALICE: In a church.

ALEX: I hate you.

ALICE: No you don't.

ALEX: I do Alice. What am I going to do? You're my mirror.

ALICE gently touches ALEX's face. She looks at him.

ALICE: Give me my ring back.

ALEX does so. He looks at her, smiles then exits. Lights focus more tightly on ALICE.

(*To audience.*) I'm reading this book at the moment, which is unusual for me because I don't do a lot of reading. Alex is the reader in our house, or at least he pretends to be. No, that's not fair, he does read a lot. He's the reader, I'm the decorator, which – as I very much like to remind him – makes me the more authentic because while he expresses the opinions of others, I express myself. I'm the artist in our house, Alex is the reader. He does quotes, I do quilts. I do birthdays, he does the bank. He remembers numbers, I remember names, although I couldn't think of a single vegetable. I don't know why I never got into fiction. But I never did. Not even at college. It just wasn't what we talked about. Me and my friends. Still isn't. But over the years I have developed a great tactic – just in case I do have to talk about a book. What I do is, I repeat verbatim, one of Alex's caffeinated rants, but I do it really quietly to one person and speak slightly tentatively. The result is that everyone thinks Alex is a bombastic git while his wife is not only extremely long-suffering but – actually – 'the real intelligence'. I love it. It drives Alex apoplectic. I haven't told him this story yet, I haven't told anyone because I've been avoiding seeing my friends because I'm avoiding formulating thoughts. Can you imagine that? Not avoiding friends, I mean I think everyone does that. But being too frightened to think. In case you can't. Can you imagine? I'm not sure. Maybe you can. Honestly, I hope you never have to experience it because it is quite simply (*Smiles.*) dreadful. And that's the only and one word for it. Dread. But I'm really not sure that you can fully appreciate that word until you do experience it. I don't know, maybe you can. We don't have any children. We wanted to. I wanted to. At least I think I did. I do now at any rate. Definitely. We play a game, in bed, a name game – you know – what we were going to call our kids. I always suggest names from the Old Testament like Moses. Alex turns puce and vetoes immediately, so I tell him fine, but my second choice is Derek. 'You're taking the piss. I can't believe you'd take the piss over something this serious!' I'm not – we can call him Del for short. Alex thinks I'm joking but I like Del. It's sweet. (*Laughs and shakes her head.*) I don't think I can explain. I can't tell you. The reality of this is… And Alex is right by the way – Max does hate him. D'you know, I think he did do it on purpose – that carpet is the only thing I've let Alex choose for the entire flat. Except for the bookshelves in the hall. Mmm. (*She draws a small circle in the air with her finger.*) It was very odd. It really was because I wasn't looking for a book. I was just walking past – about to go shopping, I remember because I had my hat on, when for some reason I stopped, put my hand out, took a book off the shelf, turned it over, looked down and there it was – one word – 'Immortality'. I mean d'you not think that's weird. I do. I really do. Immortality. If you saw that in a film you wouldn't believe it. But this is what happened and this is why, so unusually for me, I find myself reading one of Alex's books. So here's the story I want to tell. Try to tell. It's about one of the characters in the book, a woman called Agnes. And Agnes has a recurring fantasy. She's lying in bed with her husband and a stranger shows up. He's a visitor from outer space and he's come especially to offer her the chance of a new life after death. And she says, 'What about my husband?' 'Well, it's up to you,' the spaceman tells her. 'It's your choice. You can either share another life together, or you can part at the end of this one and never meet again.' But he needs a decision. Right now. Well, what can she say in front of her husband? I mean, how can she possibly admit she's tempted by the prospect of a fresh life without him? It would be like saying that there'd never been any love between them, wouldn't it? Not real love everlasting. So she always catapults. No she doesn't. She always catapults, capitulates. Capitulates. So she always capitulates – of course they want to stay together, she says.

Is it possible to become a different person?

Scene 5

The cell. DEREK is busy setting up the teleporter.

ALEX: I've got to get out of here.

DEREK: You are out of here Alex. You're having dinner with your wife.

ALEX: I missed our anniversary.

DEREK: No you didn't. You're there. Perfect continuity.

ALEX: This is a nightmare.

DEREK: It's just a story. A parallel fiction. We'll soon put an end to it. Press the button. Let's get things back to normal.

ALEX: You're joking. You are joking?

DEREK: Two people can't live one life. You said so yourself.

ALEX: I don't want to die.

DEREK: But it wouldn't be the end of the world. You of all people should understand. Your story is in safe hands. It's being told even as we speak. What are you doing now? Still at the restaurant? Driving home? Kissing Alice goodnight, walking Max? Okay. Press the button.

ALEX: Fuck the button. I don't want to die.

DEREK turns the teleporter off.

DEREK: When was the last time you were teleported?

ALEX: Derek.

DEREK: Answer the question.

ALEX: No. Really. Derek. I'm not being disrespectful, I'm not being cocky. You've got to help me.

DEREK: I'm trying Alex. When was the last time you were teleported?

ALEX: You're not hearing me…

DEREK: And you're not listening. Now think!

ALEX: I?

DEREK: *When?*

ALEX: Three weeks ago.

DEREK: So, as a sentient, self-conscious being, you are less than a month old?

ALEX: (*Definite.*) Yes. No. No.

DEREK: No, of course not. 'I'm a grown man,' your brain is telling you. 'I've lived a life. I know I have.' That's the story you're being told and that's the story you're sticking to. And so is Alex.

ALEX: I'm Alex.

Beat.

DEREK: When was the last time you woke from a dreamless sleep?

ALEX: Oh come on.

DEREK: Think man, think.

ALEX: This is ridiculous.

DEREK: Every night you're teleported. A dreamless sleep is as deep as death but you wake each morning none the wiser. Reborn. Your eyes open and your brain pulls together the threads of the tale. What's the story, it asks itself? The story is me! Our bodies might be replicated and replaced every night for all the difference it would make. We'd still be none the wiser. It's only the story that matters. Now press the button and go to sleep.

ALEX: But I don't want to go to sleep! It's an execution…a suicide. No. No! I won't do it. I want to live my own story, I want to dream my own dreams and I don't want somebody else doing it for me.

DEREK: I, I, I! Always I! I wake up in the morning; I go to work; I feel happy when things go well and I feel frustrated when they don't; I hold certain beliefs and I express various opinions; I used to like Beethoven but now I prefer Mozart; I like chocolate better than cheesecake; I enjoy walks in the countryside; I take the view that people should be kind to one another, and I feel bad if I do the wrong thing. I act, I feel, I think, I believe, I grow older and I change in other ways. But 'I' am always there at the centre of things. But what is this 'I'? The experiencer of experiences? The thinker of thoughts? The doer of deeds? Nonsense, tosh and bollocks. The simple fact is that there is no I beyond the 'I' of grammar.

ALEX: Well, do you know what I think? I think you're enjoying this. I really do. I also think you're being unbelievably patronizing.

DEREK: 'The mental processes underlying our sense of self – feelings, thoughts, memories – are scattered through different zones of the brain.' What was it? 'There is no special point of convergence. No essence, no ego, no "I".' The human brain is a story-telling machine. The self is the story. And whether you like it or not, at this very moment yours is being told.

Beat. Intimacy.

I once watched myself die.

Beat.

It was one of the first teleportations. I arrived and stepped out into the reception zone like I was stepping out of my front door. It was a big deal in those days. They were ready with drinks and everything. At first no one was aware of the malfunction. But then the message came through quick enough. Scanning and transmission had worked perfectly, of course they had, there I was soaking my reconstituted flesh in champagne – but the vaporization phase had failed. Like you, I had arrived but, at the same time, I hadn't left. They told me immediately. There was no clear protocol in those days. The difference in my case was my... (*Searching.*) original had been fatally injured by the malfunction. His cardiovascular system couldn't handle it. No one knew what to do, so they told me what had happened and let me return. It was a shock. Not so much his injuries. Just to see him. I tried to help, to console him. I told him I loved his wife. I promised him I'd take care of his daughter. I even said I'd finish the book he was writing. Because from where I stood, you see, nothing had changed; the story was the same and the story was continuing: perfect continuity. It was my wife; my child; my book. Don't despair, I told him, nothing is going to change. He so wanted to see his loved ones one last time, but he knew the distress it would cause. 'I must not,' he said. 'Let life go on as normal.' It was just me and him at the end. I held his hand. I felt so proud. His resolve. And then, then life did go on as normal. I went home. Kissed my wife, hugged my daughter. I even finished my book.

ALEX: You promised to take care of her?

DEREK: What?

ALEX: You promised to take care of Alice.

DEREK turns the teleporter on.

Why haven't you called her? This is your daughter we're talking about!

DEREK: Press the button!

ALEX: She's dying!

DEREK: You don't begin to understand, so selfish. At least I stand by my principles. I always knew you were a fake. I told her but she wouldn't listen. She never listens.

ALEX: What are you doing?

DEREK: (*Pulling ALEX towards the teleporter.*) You have to press the button!

ALEX: Get off!

An inelegant struggle, which ends when ALEX violently pushes DEREK and DEREK falls. Pulling himself together, ALEX looks at what has happened.

Fuck you.

ALEX exits and so makes his escape. Blackout.

Scene 6

Side room on a neurology ward. ALICE is sitting as in Scene 2. A long silence.

ALICE: (*Haltingly.*) Fff… Fff…

A long pause, looks at finger.

Fffff…

Looks at foot.

Foot… Fff…

Touches face.

Fff… Fff…

What? Beginning with 'A'? … Beginning with 'A', beginning with 'A':

Pause. She is concentrating but her mind is blank.

… Any word? … Any at all?… Oh this is ridiculous!

A long pause.

'S'…right… 'S'… 'S'… 'S'…

Snuffles, smiles, wipes an eye.

I'm sorry. I'm finding it hard to…

No, no way. I'm not doing the fucking animals again.

Beat.

Yes, fine. I don't mind chatting for a while.

Beat.

I'm mostly okay. I'm mostly on a level. I actually see things more clearly now, I think – in some ways. I see people more clearly, that's for sure. Although not my friends. I'm not seeing so much of my friends these days. Bastards are avoiding me! You see, I can tell it's not Alex but you can't. To me it's obvious. You're just taken in by outward appearances. How do I know? Are you married? Do you think you'd be fooled if someone came in pretending to be your wife? I don't fucking think so!

Capgras Syndrome? Oh fuck off.

Yes. I'm here because I have a tumour growing in my brain. A butterfly glioma. Actually a butterfly oligodendroglioma. Want me to spell that backwards? I know what's going on. And I can see why you might think... I understand that it sounds odd. But it's very fucking clever. He looks exactly like Alex. It's a perfect copy. But it's not just physical resemblance is it? It's not just how somebody looks and behaves. It's what they are inside. And that man, that thing, is not Alex inside.

(*Exploding.*) Yes I know perfectly fucking well what fucking Capgras Syndrome is! It's all very fucking convenient is what it is! The delusion that someone...someone you love has been replaced by an impostor.

Lights change. ALEX is now in the room with her.

ALEX: Ali...please. Look at me. Look at my face.

ALICE looks at him.

When you look at me – part of your brain is figuring out the shape of my face. Okay? Then there's another part deciding whether it's familiar, and other parts trying to analyse my expressions and the movements of my lips and my eyes...and all this triggers memories and feelings but… But what's happened… We think… I think. What's happened is that your tumour has caused a disconnection. There's a break in the circuit, between the perceptual systems, what you see, from the emotional systems, what you feel. So I'm not getting through. I can't get to the emotional core… The system shuts down. Won't let me in. So when you look at me you think, 'Well, it looks like Alex. So why don't I feel anything? I don't feel anything. So it can't be Alex.'

ALICE: No.

ALEX: Yes.

ALICE: NO!

ALEX: No, no sorry, of course you don't. You don't even think that. It's all unconscious and automatic. Your brain sets the whole thing up before you know anything about it. It sets it up. It tells you a story: 'It looks like Alex… But I don't feel anything… So it can't be Alex… So it must be an impostor.'

ALICE: Get out.

ALEX looks at his frightened wife. He reaches out to touch her face. She tenses, turns her head.

Get out.

ALEX: Ali…

ALICE: Get out of here.

ALEX: Ali, love, it's okay. It's me.

ALICE: NURSE!

During this ALEX becomes almost as distressed as ALICE.

ALEX: Alice.

ALICE: NURSE!

ALEX: We don't need the nurse Alice, it's me.

ALICE: Get your hands off me! NURSE!

ALEX: Look at me!

He holds her face tight between his hands, looks hard into her eyes. She doesn't resist. Something seems to register with ALICE. They look at one another.

ALICE: Alex? Alex!

ALICE holds ALEX to her.

ALEX: Sweetheart. Sweetheart. Sweetheart.

Suddenly, ALICE erupts into shocking violence. She lashes out grunting like a tennis player with each swipe.

ALICE: (*Swipe.*) Don't fucking sweetheart me (*Swipe.*) – get out (*Swipe.*) get out (*Swipe.*) get the fuck OUT OF HERE (*Swipe.*) I'm not (*Swipe.*) fooled. I'm not (*Swipe.*) fooled. Don't (*Swipe.*) for ONE (*Swipe.*) MINUTE (*Swipe.*) think I'm FOOLED.

With unexpected violence of his own ALEX overpowers ALICE, swinging her to the ground, but it's fear and confusion on his face, not anger. They grapple, a power struggle. If not for the context, it could seem erotic. ALEX in his desperation is disinhibited, out of control. ALICE makes an anxious sound.

No.

ALEX doesn't stop.

No. NO!

ALEX doesn't stop. ALICE makes cries for help. Suddenly someone arrives. It is DEREK. He grabs ALEX and pulls him off violently. DEREK is now face-to-face with his daughter. This was unexpected.

Dad? Dad? Dad!

ALEX: I... I'm sorry.

DEREK: (*To ALEX.*) Get out! Get out!

ALEX: I'm sorry.

DEREK: Go!

> *ALICE continues to make sounds. DEREK comforts her. ALEX exits.*

It's alright. It's alright, he's gone.

> *After a time ALICE calms. DEREK suddenly cries.*

I'm sorry. I'm so sorry.

> *Blackout.*

Scene 7

On the screen a point-of-view shot. We are running towards an open door. We see stairs. We run up them. We pass the bookshelves in the hall that ALICE described to us earlier. We run into the bathroom, the camera frantically searching. There's nobody there. Next the kitchen. No one. Stop; a thought. And now we turn to see a bedroom door ajar. And as we move towards the door the escaped ALEX enters onstage. The screen has been his point of view. The camera and onstage ALEX stop, then the door is pushed open and onstage ALEX turns to face the audience. On the screen we see another ALEX passed out on his bed. ALEX watches himself. Music is fundamental to this scene. Visual philosophy. We see on-bed ALEX from several angles. Time passes. Emotions pass. Images pass. The music guides us. We scrutinise the onstage ALEX. DEREK enters. He thought ALEX would be here. ALEX doesn't look at DEREK but he knows it's him.

ALEX: He came back hours ago. I thought you'd be with him for some reason. Not sure why. He looks pretty fucking shit doesn't he?! I didn't actually recognise him at first. It was funny. I was waiting for him, watching the flat from across the street. I don't know what I thought I was going to do. Kill him? And then he turned up. He took minutes to get his key in the door. He kept buckling over like he was going to throw up. He literally fell up the stairs. It

was pathetic. Not even comical. He left the door wide
open. I could see his feet. At the top of the stairs. He was
sitting at the top of the stairs. You know, sitting and then
he started making this sound. I didn't know what it was, it
sounded like an animal. But it was him. He was wailing.
I've only ever seen people wail on television. Arab women.
Wailing. Around a coffin. And then the sound stopped.
No. No it didn't stop. It ran out. And I looked up and
his feet weren't there. They'd disappeared and I hadn't
noticed. I hadn't been paying enough attention. And in
that moment I started to panic. A sick, physical panic: he's
done something, he's fucking done something to himself! I
ran up the stairs, and went straight to the bathroom. I don't
know why. He wasn't there. I tried the kitchen. Where is
he? Where the fuck is he? And then…then I knew where
he was. I just knew. And he was in here. Curled up like a
baby. Out for the count. He's drunk himself into oblivion.

There is a silence as they both look at the sleeper.

DEREK: I could be bound in a nut-shell and count myself a
king of infinite space.

ALEX: Were it not that I have bad dreams. Where is she?

DEREK: She's at the hospital.

ALEX: Yeah. I thought that probably…yeah…

DEREK: I did promise I'd look after her.

ALEX: Yeah.

Beat.

Well. You did exactly what he would have done.

DEREK: No. I let him down.

ALEX: Perfect continuity.

DEREK: Not for me.

ALEX: Imperfect continuity. What does it matter? No essence, no ego, no 'I'.

DEREK: (*Quickly.*) I didn't want to see her Alex. I was afraid she wouldn't recognise me. I didn't think it would be her any more.

Beat.

ALEX: We play a game, a name game – you know – what we were going to call our children. She'd always suggest names from the Old Testament like Moses or Solomon, just to wind me up. I'd tell her to stop taking the piss, so she'd say fine, but my second choice is Derek. The thing is, it's not a joke. She worships the ground you walk on.

Beat.

DEREK: She's dying Alex.

Beat.

(*Whispers.*) She's going to die.

Beat.

Quietly DEREK starts to laugh.

I've always hated the name Derek.

ALEX: (*Indicating on-screen ALEX.*) Tell him that. I think he'd really appreciate it.

ALEX exits. DEREK looks after him and then to the screen. Then to black.

Scene 8

In the hospital. ALICE is drinking from a plastic cup. Using his mobile phone, ALEX takes a picture of her.

ALICE: Are you flirting with me?

ALEX: Flirting?

ALICE: You are. You're flirting with me!

ALEX: I'm just trying to make an impression.

ALICE: (*Smiling.*) An impression. Do you know, I was proposed to in a restaurant like this.

ALEX: Really?

ALICE: Mm hm…it was beautiful. Candle-light, cocktails… the city glimmering below us… We even had a violinist. I love this place.

ALEX: Best view in town.

ALICE: I think so.

ALEX smiles, ALICE sits.

ALEX: This is where I took my wife for our first ever date.

ALICE: Your first ever date!

ALEX: It was an undercover date.

ALICE: Why undercover?

ALEX: She didn't know it was a date.

ALICE: That was very sneaky of you.

ALEX: I'm a very sneaky person.

Very quickly ALEX produces his camera phone and takes a photograph of ALICE.

ALICE: FUCK. FUCKING FUCK! YOU LITTLE SHIT! GIVE ME. FUCK. GIVE IT TO ME!

ALEX: Sorry. Sorry I didn't mean…

ALICE: Fucking give it to me.

ALEX: Sorry.

ALEX hands it over, ALICE takes it.

ALICE: (*Delighted with her new toy.*) I'm taking this back to the hospital.

ALEX: How is the hospital?

ALICE: What the fuck are you talking about? It's a fucking hospital.

Beat.

No, it's fine. More than fine. I'm being very well looked after.

ALEX: Really?

ALICE: My Dad.

ALEX: Oh.

ALICE: You know what fathers are like. Fuck. Fathers and daughters, mothers and sons.

ALEX: So they say.

ALICE: So they say.

They look at each other.

ALEX: (*Confessing.*) On the evening I proposed to my wife, I told her I'd seen a shooting star but I hadn't.

Beat.

ALICE: Why did you do that?

ALEX: I wanted to give her a romantic memory.

ALICE: That's really very sweet.

ALEX: Do you think so?

ALICE: She sounds like a lucky woman.

A moment as they stare at each other.

What are shooting stars?

ALEX: The remnants of comets.

ALICE: Yes, that's right. That is romantic.

ALEX: Is it?

ALICE: The remnants of comets. I think so.

He looks at her.

Can I ask you something? It's just that… You mustn't think I'm weird. But last night as I was lying in bed with my husband, a stranger showed up. And…it was a visitor from outer space. Now I know what that sounds like but he'd come especially to offer me the chance of a new life after death. Wow! I said, 'But what about my husband?' 'Well,' he said, 'it's up to you. It's your choice. You can either share another life together, or you can part at the end of this one and never meet again.' So what I want to ask you is, what would you have done?

ALEX: I…em…well, I would have…um…

ALICE: Would you like another drink?

ALEX: Yes. No. No. Better not. I have to give a lecture.

ALEX stands.

ALICE: What do you lecture on?

ALEX: Em…neurology.

ALICE: Really?! My husband's a neurologist. Perhaps you know him. Why are you standing up?

ALEX: (*Catching himself.*) Bad habit.

ALICE: Well sit down. You were sitting down.

ALEX: Yeah.

ALEX sits.

So your husband's a neurologist is he?

ALICE: A neurologist. Yes. Francis Crick.

ALEX: (*Has to eat a laugh.*) Oh!

ALICE: Do you know him?

ALEX: No, but I've heard of him.

ALICE: So have I. He has an astonishing hypothesis but I can't remember what it is.

ALEX can't help himself, he laughs.

Are you laughing at me?

ALEX: (*Smiling.*) No...

ALICE becomes agitated.

ALICE: Yes you are. You're fucking laughing at me! FUCK!

ALEX: Honestly Alice I wasn't.

ALICE: FUCK! FUCK!

ALEX: I wasn't... It's just that I know what his hypothesis is.

ALICE: LIAR!

ALEX: He says... He says that you're nothing but a bundle of neurons.

ALICE: That's what my husband says?

ALEX: Yes.

ALICE: Fuck. And what do you say?

Beat.

ALEX: I say the same thing.

ALICE: Do you? Do you really? Just a bundle of neurons? Well that's sad. I mean I'm sorry. But it is, isn't it. It's sad. I mean. And suspicious. All sounds a bit too Buddhist if you ask me. God I hate chanting... I had this boyfriend once. James Carson. Never stopped chanting. Om Mane Padme Hum... What a FAKE!

ALEX: Really?

ALICE: A complete charlatan. Can't believe I fell for it. Fuck. I like my husband. I can never remember what he says but I like him. And it's not because he's always boring, he's not. Not always. Not to me anyway. God he rants. BOMBASTIC GIT! I'm the real intelligence, and I do listen... I do! I always listen!... I mean, I do quilts and he does quotes which makes me more authentic. I do names and... And... He's my mirror... Isn't that beautiful? It's because of my butterfly glioma. I have a butterfly glioma. Isn't that beautiful?

Moments pass as ALEX stares at his beautiful wife.

ALEX: Yes. Can I ask *you* a question Alice?

ALICE considers.

ALICE: One.

ALEX: Imagine your visitor from outer space joined us now at this table. He makes his offer of another life beyond death, and gives you the choice. You can either choose for your husband to join you or you can decide that, at the end of this life, you should part company never to meet again. What would you do?

Beat.

ALICE: Truthfully?

ALEX: Truthfully.

Beat.

ALICE: I'd go it alone. Wouldn't you?

Beat. ALEX stares at his wife.

One lifetime's enough, however much you love someone.

ALICE looks at ALEX. Then she takes off her wedding-ring and holds it out to ALEX. She gently smiles so that we see the old ALICE. Lights close down to the ring and ALEX. We stay like this, and so enter Scene 9.

Scene 9

ALEX at thought. The screen represents the bundle of thoughts and feeling in ALEX's brain which we do not normally see. ALEX's face appears on the screen and begins to speak the VO lines. ALEX's face is intercut with images of ALICE and even of DEREK. The impression should be of a brain soliloquy and should mix images and inner voices with outer voice.

'VO' indicates ALEX's recorded voiceover, sometimes seen on the screen; 'VO (2)' indicates a second voice in ALEX's head, also a recorded voiceover; ALICE and DEREK are also recorded voiceovers.

ALEX takes off his wedding-ring and considers it.

VO: Okay, I think we should make a start now.

VO (2): Okay.

VO: (*As if prompting.*) Thank you. Let's make a start.

VO (2): Okay.

> *Beat.*

> So look at me.

VO (2): So look at me.

VO *and* VO (2): Look at my face.

VO (2): Look. The eyes. The mouth. What do you see?

VO: What do you see?

VO (2): A bony box and mechanical things.

VO: So what do you see?

VO (2): You catch my gleaming eye and see –

VO: (*Whispers.*) A person.

VO (2): *A person.*

VO: An entire universe, an infinite space.

VO (2): A person.

VO: This is the normal intuition. But look…

VO (2): Look into the space behind the face.

VO: Now what do you see?

VO (2): Meat. A lump of meat.

VO: What do you see?

VO (2): Butterflies.

VO: What do you see?

VO (2): A lump of meat.

VO: There's no one there.

VO (2): There's nobody home.

    Blackout on stage. Silence.

VO: (*Whispers from the darkness.*) No essence. No ego. No 'I'.

VO (2): No essence. No Ego. No 'I'.

VO: A voice, that's all.

VO (2): Just a voice.

VO: Just a voice telling stories.

VO (2): And when the voice stops…

    Beat. Lights up. ALEX lets out emotion, then silence.

ALICE (VO): It's a kind of liberation.

    Pause. ALEX takes the wedding-ring from ALICE. ALICE gently exits.

VO: So…

ALEX: So…

VO: So, there is no central core… No inner 'I'… We are divided and discontinuous. Feelings, thoughts, memories…

ALEX: Are scattered through different zones of the brain.

VO *and* ALEX: There's no special point of convergence.

VO: No soul-pilot.

ALEX: No soul-pilot working the controls.

VO *and* ALEX: We come together in a work of fiction.

ALEX: The human brain is a story-telling machine.

VO: The self is a story…

ALEX: But who tells the story of the self?

VO: Who thunders the thunder?

VO (2): Who rains the rain?

ALEX attempts to become the lecturer from Scene 1.

ALEX: Like the surface of the earth, the brain is pretty much mapped.

VO: I am the story.

ALEX: There are no secret compartments inaccessible to the surgeon's knife…

VO: I am the story.

ALEX: Or the gaze of the brain scanner.

VO: I am the story.

ALEX: There's nothing you can't touch or squeeze, weigh and measure… No ghost in the machine… Just a machine…

ALICE (VO): (*A definite intrusion.*) So how does meat become mind?

ALEX: I don't know.

VO: I don't care.

ALEX: I don't know.

VO: I don't care.

ALEX: I...

> *A thunderclap. Time stops again. ALEX stops. As the thunder rolls away...*

VO: I am the story.

> *Beat.*

VO (2): Let's go back.

VO: Yes.

VO (2): Let's make a start

VO: Back to the illusion.

VO (2): The intuition.

VO: The ego.

VO (2): The observing 'I'.

VO: The ghost.

ALICE (VO *and on screen*): The ghost in the machine.

DEREK (VO): Poor drowned soul.

ALICE (VO *and on screen*): The promise of another life.

DEREK (VO *and on screen*): Beyond death.

ALICE (VO): With me.

VO (2): Or without.

ALICE (VO): Part company?

VO (2): Never to meet again.

ALICE (VO): It's your decision.

VO (2): What can I say?

ALICE (VO): What would you do?

ALEX: I would...

ALICE (VO): Truthfully.

ALEX: I don't know.

ALICE (VO): Good choice.

ALEX: But I... [haven't given you an answer.]

ALICE (VO): Very good choice.

ALEX: To be with you?

ALICE (VO): Or without.

VO (2): (*Something dawns.*) ... Yes.

VO: 'For put them side by side,
   The one the other will include,
   With ease, and you, beside.'

ALEX: And you beside.

ALICE (VO): He sent you his love by the way.

ALEX: His love?

ALICE (VO): Mmm. Perhaps you should call him.

VO: The illusion is irresistible...

ALEX: The illusion. The ego.

   Beat.

VO: A little magical thinking. A little spooky stuff.

DEREK (VO): It makes the world go round.

VO: It makes the world go round.

   Still holding his wedding-ring.

ALEX: Behind the face. What do you see?

VO (2): The impenetrable darkness?

VO: No. You don't.

ALEX: You see a person.

VO: The best view in town.

Holds up wedding-ring; inspects it. Lights change suddenly. Time is frozen.

ALICE (VO): I'd go it alone. Wouldn't you?

VO (2): Would you?

ALICE: (*Silence says 'yes'.*)

ALEX: So, it's just the one lifetime?

ALICE (VO): Afraid so. Better make the most of it.

ALEX: I love this place.

ALICE (VO): Best view in town.

A shooting star flies across the screen. DEREK enters with the teleporter.

DEREK (VO): And each time you travel there's perfect continuity. Perfect continuity between the person dematerialising and the person re-emerging. Perfect continuity of memory, emotion and thought. Perfect continuity.

DEREK exits.

VO: It wouldn't be the end of the world.

DEREK (VO): Going anywhere nice?

VO (2): It's the story that matters.

DEREK (VO): I'm going to have dinner with my daughter.

VO: What do you see?

DEREK (VO): My daughter.

VO: Behind the face.

DEREK (VO): My daughter.

VO (2): What do you see?

DEREK (VO): I'll see you tomorrow.

VO: Behind the face.

DEREK (VO): A dreamless sleep.

VO: Behind the face.

DEREK (VO): I'll see you tomorrow.

VO (2): Behind the face.

DEREK (VO): Ready?

VO: Behind the face.

DEREK: Ready?

VO: Can you let go of the illusion?

Images on the screen freeze. Music stops.

Wait.

ALEX looks up slightly. Very gently he smiles.

ALEX: Happy Anniversary Alice.

Beat. Then ALEX presses the green button. The screen suddenly runs hundreds of images, mapping ALEX's mind and the history of his relationship with ALICE. Sound and lights intensify around ALEX as the scanners do their work. A crescendo to a final image: on stage, ALEX; on screen, his photograph of ALICE from Scene 8. Stop. Then suddenly, blackout.

CPSIA information can be obtained
at www.ICGtesting.com
Printed in the USA
LVHW021110250721
693626LV00012B/1315